Making Joyful Noises

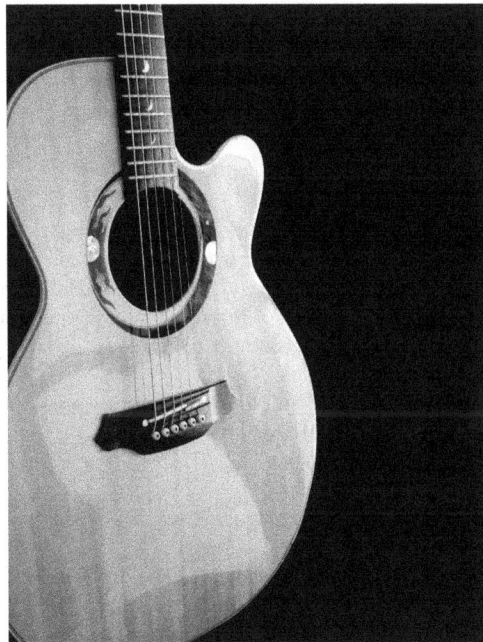

Mastering the Fundamentals of Music

Contents

Introduction

Make a joyful noise unto God, all ye lands: Sing forth the honour of his name: make his praise glorious. ~ Ps. 66.1-2 (KJV)

Our God, the God and Father of our Lord Jesus Christ, is worthy of praise. His command in Psalm 66 is to make a joyful noise, that is, to make music for the glory of his name. The Lord inhabits the praises of his people (Ps. 22.3), and we ought to learn to praise him with excellence, skill, and passion. Our infinitely worthy God deserves our best and highest praise.

This booklet contains the basic fundamentals of music. Each of these fundamentals is explained briefly, not with an emphasis on theory alone. The focus is on *learning* the fundamentals so you can *practice* using that knowledge to master them. I encourage you to spend much time seeking to understand how music works (the fancy term for this is "music theory"), so you can know not just *how* to play a chord or rhythm, but also to understand *what is happening* and *why* you are playing it. This is the key to becoming truly excellent in music for the sake of giving God our highest praise.

Nothing is assumed in this book. It is written from a very non-technical standpoint, although it is a treasure of music theory. Focus on the fundamentals, learn the theory, and translate the theory into practice. And don't forget; practice doesn't make perfect; only *right practice* makes perfect. Concentrate on learning each technique slowly, and concentrate on mastering each fundamental as you go. Take your time, though. Only those who are natural geniuses can do things perfectly the first time, and even they have to practice to keep up their skill. God will honor your discipline and effort.

Above all else, please remember the reason for all of your hard work at developing your music skill–your love for our triune God, Father, Son, and Holy Spirit. Obey him by trying to make a *joyful* noise to the Lord, and seek to make each practice session fun and relaxing. Never forget *why* you are bothering to learn about scales, rhythms, keys, and beats and such. We are learning the rhythms for a remarkable reason–the high praise of our immortal and wonderful God!

May the Lord bless your efforts as you master music to make our Master good music!

Don L. Davis

Chord Fingering

The diagram at the right represents the top end of the guitar fingerboard. The horizontal lines represent the Nut and Frets 1, 2, and 3. The vertical lines represent the six strings.

Fingering for the Left Hand

Numerals (0, 1, 2, 3, 4) are sometimes indicated in chord diagrams, appearing either above the Nut-line or adjacent to the black marks (♦). These numerals denote fingering for the left hand and are to be read as follows:

0 - Play an open string with right hand. Do not touch or press it with your left.
1 - Press the string at mark (♦) with the first finger.
2 - Press the string at mark (♦) with the second finger.
3 - Press the string at mark (♦) with the third finger.
4 - Press the string at mark (♦) with the fourth finger.

The strings not marked are to remain silent–not picked or strummed with the right hand. Open strings (marked 0) are of course picked or strummed.

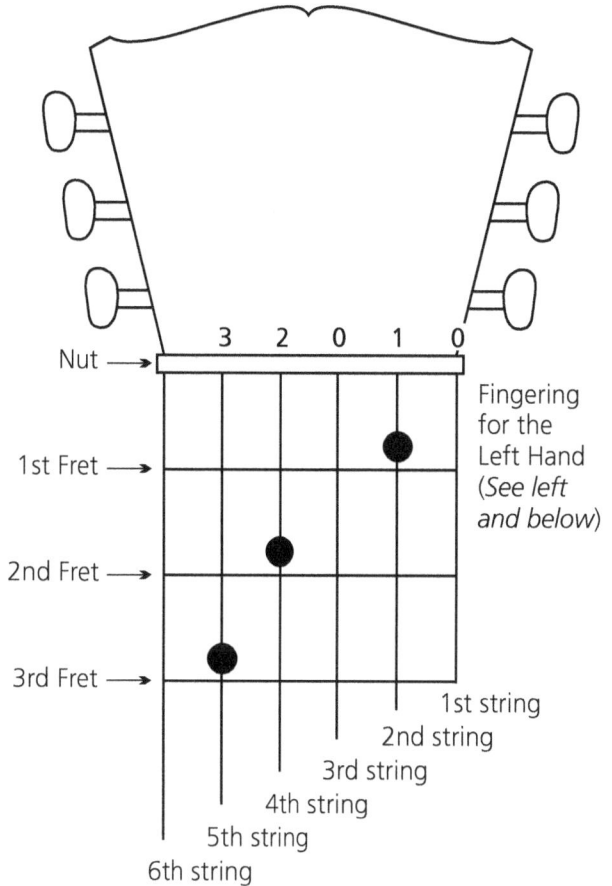

The diagram above specifies that the first and third strings are to be played as open strings, while the sixth string is not to be played at all. Also, only three fingers of the left hand are to be used to form the chord. It happens to be a C chord. In many chord charts (including those in this book), it would look like this:

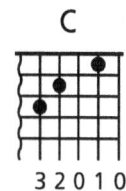

Principal Chords and Relative Minor Sets
for the Guitar's Moveable Chords

Key	3 Principal Chords			Relative Minor		
	I	IV	V7	VIm	IIm	III7
C	C	F	G7	Am	Dm	E7
	3 2 0 1 0	3 2 1 1	3 2 0 0 0 1	0 2 3 1 0	0 0 2 4 1	0 2 0 1 0 0
G	G	C	D7	Em	Am	B7
	3 2 0 0 0 4	3 2 0 1 0	0 0 2 1 3	0 2 3 0 0 0	0 2 3 1 0	2 1 3 0 4
D	D	G	A7	Bm	Em	F#7
	0 0 1 3 2	3 2 0 0 0 4	0 1 1 1 3	3 4 2 1	0 2 3 0 0 0	3 2 1 0
A	A	D	E7	F#m	Bm	C#7
	0 2 1 3 0	0 0 1 3 2	0 2 0 1 0 0	3 1 1 1	3 4 2 1	3 2 4 1
E	E	A	B7	C#m	F#m	G#7 (A♭7)
	0 2 3 1 0 0	0 2 1 3 0	2 1 3 0 4	2 1 3 0	3 1 1 1	1 1 1 3

Scales

The Circle of Fifths

Nothing is more important for a budding musician than to memorize the essential elements of music theory. Don't fret, though; this isn't hard. You will learn that if you master a few simple rules of music theory, you will be able to apply them in numerous musical contexts. In music theory, a little knowledge goes a long way!

The Circle of Fifths (illustrated below) is a wonderful way to memorize the critical fifth (as well as fourth) degree of a key scale, depending on which direction you go. For example, beginning at "C," if you go counterclockwise, you will encounter "G," which is the **fifth** of "C." "D" is the **fifth** of "G," and so on. Again, beginning at "C" and going clockwise, you will encounter "F" which is the **fourth** of "C." "B flat" is the **fourth** of "F", and so on. The rule is simple: for any scale on the circle, its **fourth** is on the *right* and its **fifth** is on the *left*.

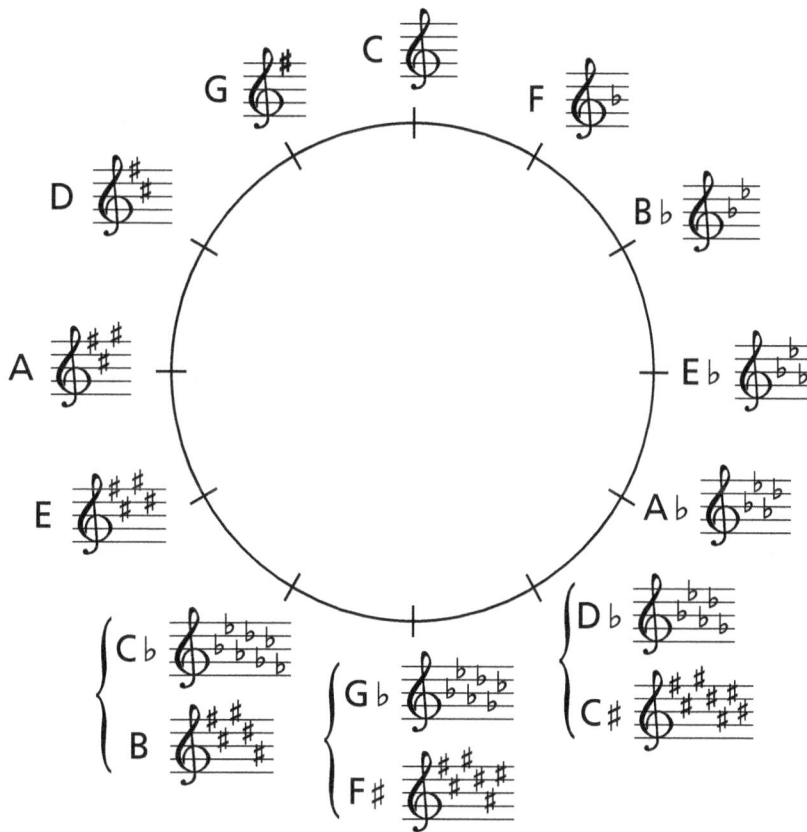

Pitches: Sharps and Flats. Below are two acrostics to help you memorize the Major keys, both sharps and flats.

For the Sharps (G-D-A-E-B-F♯-C♯): "**G**oats **D**on't **A**lways **E**at **B**arley **F**ood, **C**harlie!"

For the Flats (F-B♭-E♭-A♭-D♭-G♭-C♭): "**F**erocious **B**ears **E**at **A**ardvarks, **D**ucks, **G**eese, **C**hickens!"

Scales, continued

Minor Scales

Every one of the major scales has a corresponding *relative minor* scale that shares the same key signature. You can find the starting note of a major scale's relative minor scale by going up to the sixth degree of that major scale. Thus, the relative minor of C major is A minor.

Harmonic and Melodic Minor Scales

The relative minor scales referred to above are known as *natural minor* scales because they occur naturally, without deviating from their key signatures. These scales are commonly altered to form *harmonic minor* and *melodic minor* scales. The harmonic minor scale is formed by raising the seventh degree of a natural minor.

Major Key	Number of Sharps	Relative Minor
C Major	0	A Minor
G Major	1 (F♯)	E Minor
D Major	2 (F♯, C♯)	B Minor
A Major	3 (F♯, C♯, G♯)	F♯ Minor
E Major	4 (F♯, C♯, G♯, D♯)	C♯ Minor
B Major	5 (F♯, C♯, G♯, D♯, A♯)	G♯ Minor
F♯ Major	6 (F♯, C♯, G♯, D♯, A♯, E♯)	D♯ Minor
C♯ Major	7 (F♯, C♯, G♯, D♯, A♯, E♯, B♯)	A♯ Minor
	Number of Flats	
F Major	1 (B♭)	D Minor
B♭ Major	2 (B♭, E♭)	G Minor
E♭ Major	3 (B♭, E♭, A♭)	C Minor
A♭ Major	4 (B♭, E♭, A♭, D♭)	F Minor
D♭ Major	5 (B♭, E♭, A♭, D♭, G♭)	B♭ Minor
G♭ Major	6 (B♭, E♭, A♭, D♭, G♭, C♭)	E♭ Minor
C♭ Major	7 (B♭, E♭, A♭, D♭, G♭, C♭, F♭)	A♭ Minor

Chord Accompaniment Guide
Principals, Relative Minors, and Alternate Chords

Key	3 Principal Chords			Relative Minor			Alternate Chords					
	I	IV	V7	VIm	IIm	III7						
C	C 32010	F 3211	G7 320001	Am 02310	Dm 00241	E7 020100	C6 (Am7) 2314	C dim 1324	C Aug 3211	F6 0211	Am6 2314	Dm6 0201
G	G 320004	C 32010	D7 00213	Em 023000	Am 02310	B7 21304	G6 (Em7) 320000	G dim 1324	G Aug 1004	C6 2314	Em6 023040	Am6 2314
F	F 3211	Bb 2341	C7 32410	Dm 00241	Gm 0333	A7 01113	F6 (Dm7) 0211	F dim 0102	F Aug 4231	Bb6 3333	Dm6 0201	Gm6 1333
D	D 00132	G 320004	A7 01113	Bm 3421	Em 023000	F#7 3210	D6 (Bm7) 00321	D dim 0102	D Aug 0231	G6 320000	Bm6 2314	Em6 023040
Bb	Bb 2341	Eb 3121	F7 1324	Gm 0333	Cm 3421	D7 00213	Bb6 (Gm7) 3333	Bb dim 1324	Bb Aug 4231	Eb6 1203	Gm6 1333	Cm6 1214
A	A 02130	D 00132	E7 020100	F#m 3111	Bm 3421	C#7 3241	A6 (F#m7) 3333	A dim 1324	A Aug 4231	D6 00321	F#m6 1333	Bm6 2314
Eb	Eb 3121	Ab 3211	Bb7 1113	Cm 3421	Fm 3111	G7 320001	Eb6 (Cm7) 1203	Eb dim 1324	Eb Aug 100	Ab6 1111	Cm6 1214	Fm6 0111
E	E 023100	A 02130	B7 21304	C#m 2130	F#m 3111	G#7 (Ab7) 1113	E6 (C#m7) 023140	E dim 1324	E Aug 3120	A6 3333	C#m6 1214	F#m6 1333
Ab	Ab 3211	Db 3121	Eb7 1324	Fm 3111	Bbm 3421	C7 32410	Ab6 (Fm7) 1111	Ab dim 0102	Ab Aug 120	Db6 2314	Fm6 0111	Bbm6 2314
B	B 2341	E 023100	F#7 3210	G#m (Abm) 3111	C#m 2130	D#7 (Eb7) 1324	B6 (Abm7) 3333	B dim 0102	B Aug 2100	E6 023140	G#m6 (Abm6) 1333	C#m6 1214
Db	Db 3121	Gb 3211	Ab7 1113	Bbm 3421	Ebm 3421	F7 1324	Db6 (Bbm7) 2314	Db dim 1324	Db Aug 3211	Gb6 2314	Bbm6 (A#m6) 2314	Ebm6 1324
F#	F# 3211	B 2341	C#7 3241	D#m (Ebm) 3241	G#m (Abm) 3111	A#7 (Bb7) 1113	F#6 (Ebm7) 2314	F# dim 1324	F# Aug 4231	B6 3333	D#m6 (Ebm) 1324	G#m6 (Abm6) 1333

Chord Building Chart

Chord Type	Scale Degrees Used
Major	Root, 3rd, 5th
Minor	Root, ♭3rd, 5th
Diminished	Root, ♭3rd, ♭5th, ♭♭7th
Augmented	Root, 3rd, ♮5th
Dominant Seventh	Root, 3rd, 5th, ♭7th
Minor Seventh	Root, ♭3rd, 5th, ♭7th
Major Seventh	Root, 3rd, 5th, maj. 7th
Major Sixth	Root, 3rd, 5th, 6th
Minor Sixth	Root, ♭3rd, 5th, 6th
Seventh ♯5th	Root, 3rd, ♯5th, ♭7th
Major 7th ♭3rd	Root, ♭3rd, 5th, maj. 7th
Minor 7th ♭5th	Root, ♭3rd, ♭5th, ♭7th
Seventh Suspended 4th	Root, 4th, 5th, ♭7th
Ninth	Root, 3rd, 5th, ♭7th, 9th
Minor Ninth	Root, ♭3rd, 5th, ♭7th, 9th
Major Ninth	Root, 3rd, 5th, maj. 7th, 9th
Ninth Augmented 5th	Root, 3rd, ♯5th, ♭7th, 9th
Ninth Flatted 5th	Root, 3rd, ♭5th, ♭7th, 9th
Seventh ♭9	Root, 3rd, 5th, ♭7th, ♭9th
Augmented Ninth	Root, 3rd, 5th, ♭7th, ♯9th
9/6	Root, 3rd, 5th, 6th, 9th
Eleventh	Root, 3rd, 5th, ♭7th, 9th, 11th
Augmented Eleventh	Root, 3rd, 5th, ♭7th, 9th, ♯11th
Thirteenth	Root, 3rd, 5th, ♭7th, 9th, 11th, 13th
Thirteenth ♭9	Root, 3rd, 5th, ♭7th, ♭9th, 11th, 13th
Thirteenth ♭9 ♭5	Root, 3rd, ♭5th, ♭7th, ♭9th, 11th, 13th

Note: To arrive at scale degrees above 1 octave (i.e., 9th, 11th, 13th) continue your scale up 2 octaves and keep numbering. The 2nd scale degree is the 9th tone as you begin your second octave.

Universal Key (scale degrees)

| 1 | (♭9) ♭2 | 2 | (9) (♯9) ♯2 ♭3 | 3 | 4 | (11) (♯11) ♯4 ♭5 | 5 | ♯5 ♭6 | 6 | (13) | ♭7 | 7 | 1 (8) |

The Function of Chords

The Roman numerals in this chart indicate the degree of the scale of the key on which the chord is built. For example, a II7 in the key of E♭ is built on the second scale step which is F.

IM7	Establishes the key center, doesn't need to progress.
V7	Progresses to I (down a 5th).
IImi7	Progresses to V (down a 5th) or to ♭II (down a ½ step).

VImi7	Substitute for I, progresses to II (down 5th) or to ♭VI (down ½ step).
VI7	Progresses to II (down 5th) or to ♭VI (down ½ step).
IIImi7	Substitute for I, often follows V7, progresses to VI (down 5th) or to ♭III (down ½ step).
III7	Progresses to VI (down 5th) or to ♭III7 (down ½ step).
II7	Progresses to V (down 5th) or to ♭II (down ½ step).
I7	Progresses to IV (down 5th) for temporary key change for relief.
IVM7	Temporary key center for relief from original key.
Vmi7	IImi7 of IV progresses to I7 (down a 5th) and then to IV.
VIIø7	Progresses to I, substitute for V.
IVmi7	Transitional chord between IVM7 and return to I, or between IImi7 and I.

♭VII7	Transitional chord between IVmi7 and I, may progress to ♭III (down 5th).
♭III7	Substitute for VI7, progresses to II (down ½ step) or to ♭VI (down 5th).
♭VI7	Substitute for II7, progresses to V (down ½ step) or to ♭II (down 5th).
♭II7	Substitute for V7, progresses to I (down ½ step).

Key: 7 - Dominant 7th; M7 - Major 7th; mi7 - minor 7th

Table of Keys

The *Table of Keys* can be used to find the notes of any chord or scale in any key, and to transpose melodies and chord progressions. The table shows the relationship between the major scale (DO RE MI FA SO LA TI DO) and the chromatic scale (which divides the octave into twelve equal half steps) in each of the twelve major keys.

one octave (twelve half-steps)

	DO		RE		MI	FA		SO		LA		TI	DO
Major Scale	DO		RE		MI	FA		SO		LA		TI	DO
		whole		whole	half		whole		whole		whole	half	
Universal Key (scale degrees)	1 (tonic)	(b9)/b2	2	(9)(#9)/#2/b3	3	4	(11)(#11)/#4/b5	5	#5/b6	6 (13)	b7	7	1 (8) octave
Key of C	C	Db	D	D#/Eb	E	F	F#/Gb	G	G#/Ab	A	Bb	B	C
Key of Db	Db	Ebb	Eb	E/Fb	F	Gb	G/Abb	Ab	A/Bbb	Bb	Cb	C	Db
Key of D	D	Eb	E	E#/F	F#	G	G#/Ab	A	A#/Bb	B	C	C#	D
Key of Eb	Eb	Fb	F	F#/Gb	G	Ab	A/Bbb	Bb	B/Cb	C	Db	D	Eb
Key of E	E	F	F#	Fx/G	G#	A	A#/Bb	B	B#/C	C#	D	D#	E
Key of F	F	Gb	G	G#/Ab	A	Bb	B/Cb	C	C#/Db	D	Eb	E	F
Key of F#	F#	G	G#	Gx/A	A#	B	B#/C	C#	Cx/D	D#	E	E#	F#
Key of Gb	Gb	Abb	Ab	A/Bbb	Bb	Cb	C/Dbb	Db	D/Ebb	Eb	Fb	F	Gb
Key of G	G	Ab	A	A#/Bb	B	C	C#/Db	D	D#/Eb	E	F	F#	G
Key of Ab	Ab	Bbb	Bb	B/Cb	C	Db	D/Ebb	Eb	E/Fb	F	Gb	G	Ab
Key of A	A	Bb	B	B#/C	C#	D	D#/Eb	E	E#/F	F#	G	G#	A
Key of Bb	Bb	Cb	C	C#/Db	D	Eb	E/Fb	F	F#/Gb	G	Ab	A	Bb
Key of B	B	C	C#	Cx/D	D#	E	E#/F	F#	Fx/G	G#	A	A#	B
Universal Key (chord function)	I	bII	II	bIII	III	IV	bV	V	bVI	VI	bVII	VII	I

The Universal Key uses a number rather than a letter to name each note of the major scale (DO = 1, RE = 2, MI = 3, etc.). By thinking of the notes of a chord or melody as numbers, it is easy to find the corresponding notes in any key. The Universal Key is used by musicians as an easy-to-understand system that simplifies communicating and playing all styles of music.

Scales, Key Signatures, and Chords

Understanding the Music Scale

Because its sound is so familiar, the major scale has been used for centuries as the standard musical reference scale. The characteristic sound of the major scale (or any other scale) is created by its structure (order of whole and half steps), which is the same in all keys. In the Universal Key system, the tones of the major scale are expressed as numbers: DO=1, RE=2, MI=3, FA=4, SO=5, LA=6, TI=7, DO=1(8). Non-major tones are expressed in terms of their relationship to the major scale (E♭ in the key of C is ♭3; A♭ in the key of D is ♭5). Chord tones which are second octave extensions of seventh chords are listed in parentheses (9, ♯11, etc.). The notes of any chord or scale may be found in any key by comparing the formula for any chord or scale from the *Chord Building Chart* (or other reference source) to the *Table of Keys*.

The following example shows how one scale (G major) relates to the Universal Key, the piano keyboard, and the treble staff.

Major Scale

DO		RE		MI	FA		SO		LA		TI	DO

Universal Key

| 1 | (♭9) ♭2 | 2 | (9)(♯9) ♯2 ♭3 | 3 | 4 | (11)(♯11) ♯4 ♭5 | 5 | ♯5 ♭6 | 6 | (13) | ♭7 | 7 | 1 (8) |

Key of G

G	A♭	A	A♯/B♭	B	C	C♯/D♭	D	D♯/E♭	E	F	F♯	G

G Major Scale (on treble staff)

```
        G   A   B   C   D   E   F♯  G
        1   2   3   4   5   6   7  1(8)
```

G Major Scale (on keyboard)

```
        G A B C D E F♯ G
        1 2 3 4 5 6 7 1(8)
```

Key Signatures

Every key signature describes a major key (capital letters) and its relative minor key (small letters). These scales have the same notes but begin on different tonics. In a key signature, sharps and flats name (by the line or space on which they fall) the notes of the C major scale which must be altered to play in the designated key.

Finding Chords and Scales

The notes of any chord or scale may be found in any key by comparing the formula for any chord or scale from the *Chord Building Chart* to the *Table of Keys*.

To find the notes of any chord, for example, Fm7:

1. Use the *Chord Building Chart* (or other reference source) to find the chord formula (minor seventh - ♭1/♭3/5/♭7).

2. Look on the *Table of Keys* for the Key (F).

3. Find the notes in that key that correspond to the numbers of the chord formula (1=F, ♭3=A♭, 5=C, ♭7=E♭).

Key of F

(F)	G♭	G	G♯/A♭ (A♭)	A	B♭	B/C♭	(C)	C♯/D♭	D	(E♭)	E	F

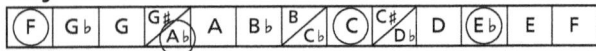

Universal Key

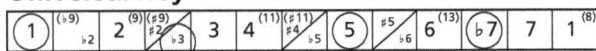

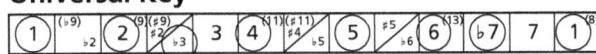

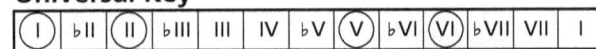

(1)	(♭9) ♭2	2	(9)(♯9) ♯2/♭3	3	4	(11)(♯11) ♯4/♭5	(5)	♯5/♭6	6	(13) ♭7	7	1 (8)

To find the notes of any scale or mode, follow the same steps, for example, B♭ dorian, which has the formula: 1/2/♭3/4/5/6/♭7/1.

Key of F

(B♭)	C♭	(C)	C♯/D♭	D	(E♭)	E/F♭	(F)	F♯/G♭	(G)	(A♭)	A	(B♭)

Universal Key

(1)	(♭9) ♭2	(2)	(9)(♯9) ♯2/♭3	3	(4)	(♯11)(♯11) ♯4/♭5	(5)	♯5/♭6	(6)	(13) ♭7	7	(1) (8)

Transposing Chord Progressions

Roman numerals (I, IV, V, etc.) are used to indicate major chords built off any scale degree. Other chords (minor, seventh, etc.) are represented by a Roman numeral followed by the abbreviation for that chord type (IVm would be a minor chord with the fourth degree of the major scale as its root). The Roman numeral system is used extensively by working musicians for writing chord charts.

For example, transpose this progression from the key of C to the key of F:

C/G7/C/C/Am/D7/G7/C

Key of C (original key)

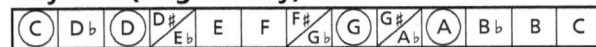

(C)	D♭	(D)	D♯/E♭	E	F	F♯/G♭	(G)	G♯/A♭	(A)	B♭	B	C

Key of F (new key)

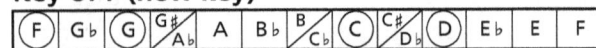

(F)	G♭	(G)	G♯/A♭	A	B♭	B/C♭	(C)	C♯/D♭	(D)	E♭	E	F

Universal Key

(I)	♭II	(II)	♭III	III	IV	♭V	(V)	♭VI	(VI)	♭VII	VII	I

1. Find the letter names of all the chord types in the original progression (C, G, A, and D).

2. Find the numerals of the Universal Key that correspond to each chord (C=I, G=V, A=VI, D=II), then add the chord type suffix (m, 7, dim, etc.). Written in the Universal Key, the progression would be **I/V7/I/I/VIm/II7/V7/I**. (Variation: sometimes lower case Roman numerals are used to indicate minor chords [ex. vi instead of VIm]).

3. Find the chords of the new key that correspond to the numerals of the progression. (I=F, V=C, VI=D, II=G).

4. Write out the progression in the new key, adding the appropriate chord types. Progression in key of F:

F/C7/F/F/Dm/G7/C7/F

The Great Staff

The lines and spaces of the Great Staff take their names from the notes of the C major scale which fall on them. Notes which are outside the C major scale are designated by accidentals: sharps (♯) raise notes one half step; flats (♭) lower notes one half step; double sharps (x) raise notes a whole step; double flats (♭♭) lower notes a whole step; naturals (♮) cancel the effect of other accidentals.

Key Transposition Worksheet

Example:

Original Key	Ⓐ	B♭	B	B♯/C	Ⓒ♯	Ⓓ	D♯/E♭	Ⓔ	E♯/F	Ⓕ♯	G	G♯	Ⓐ
Universal Key	I	(♭9) ♭2	II	(♯9) ♯2/♭3	III	IV	(♯11) ♯4/♭5	V	♯5/♭6	VI	♭7	VII	I
New Key	Ⓖ	A♭	A	A♯/B♭	Ⓑ	Ⓒ	C♯/D♭	Ⓓ	D♯/E♭	Ⓔ	F	F♯	Ⓖ

Original Key													
Universal Key	I	(♭9) ♭2	II	(♯9) ♯2/♭3	III	IV	(♯11) ♯4/♭5	V	♯5/♭6	VI	♭7	VII	I
New Key													

Original Key													
Universal Key	I	(♭9) ♭2	II	(♯9) ♯2/♭3	III	IV	(♯11) ♯4/♭5	V	♯5/♭6	VI	♭7	VII	I
New Key													

Finding and Transposing One Chord Form to Another Chord Form
Don L. Davis

1. Find the **root tone** (i.e., the pitch or key the song is in). If you are using the guitar, find the key center (i.e., root tone) on either the fifth or the sixth string; search around and determine the tone in which the song is being played or sung.

2. Find the **key center**; this is important. Songs are done in either the major key (based on the first note of the scale) or in the minor key (based on the sixth note of the scale). Determine if the song you are playing is done in a major or minor pitch.

3. Based on your finding the root tone, now determine what **chord form** will be most simple to play this song with. Remember, the movable chord forms are simple and remain the same all the way up the guitar (that is the reason why a capo works)! Here is the formula below for determining what chord form to use:

   a. The C chord fingering family is based on the FIFTH STRING ROOT TONE. For example, if you found the root tone on the fifth string at the seventh fret, you would place your capo on the fourth fret, and then use C fingering to use the principal chords, the relative minors, and alternate chord fingerings that you would use normally when playing in the key of C.

   b. The A chord fingering family is based on the FIFTH STRING ROOT TONE.

   c. The G chord fingering family is based on the SIXTH STRING ROOT TONE.

   d. The E chord fingering family is based on the SIXTH STRING ROOT TONE.

   e. The D chord fingering family is based on the FOURTH STRING ROOT TONE. For the D chord fingering family use, you must make sure that you can find the root tone on the FOURTH string in a position low enough on the fretboard to allow you to use the D chord fingering comfortably. *As a rule of thumb, if you cannot play the fingering family comfortably, you should switch to another fingering family to play your song.* Also, you want to use a fingering that allows for the most appropriate and biggest sound you can get.

   f. By the way, one way to find this out is the **rule of seven.** This rule says that if you go down seven frets on the next largest string from the root tone, you will find that tone on that string. Use this rule when determining just where is the best place for you to place your capo, and which fingering family you will use for a particular song.

   g. Remember the forms: (Major moveable forms – E, G, A, C, or D; moveable minor forms – C♯m, Em, F♯, Am, Bm). Look on the chart for details.

4. Once you've determined the root tone, the chord form, and settled on a fingering family, place **the capo on the appropriate fret** to take advantage of the form.

5. Identify **the pitch,** and determine what principal chords and relative minors you need to use in this particular form.

Musical Notation for the Guitar Fretboard

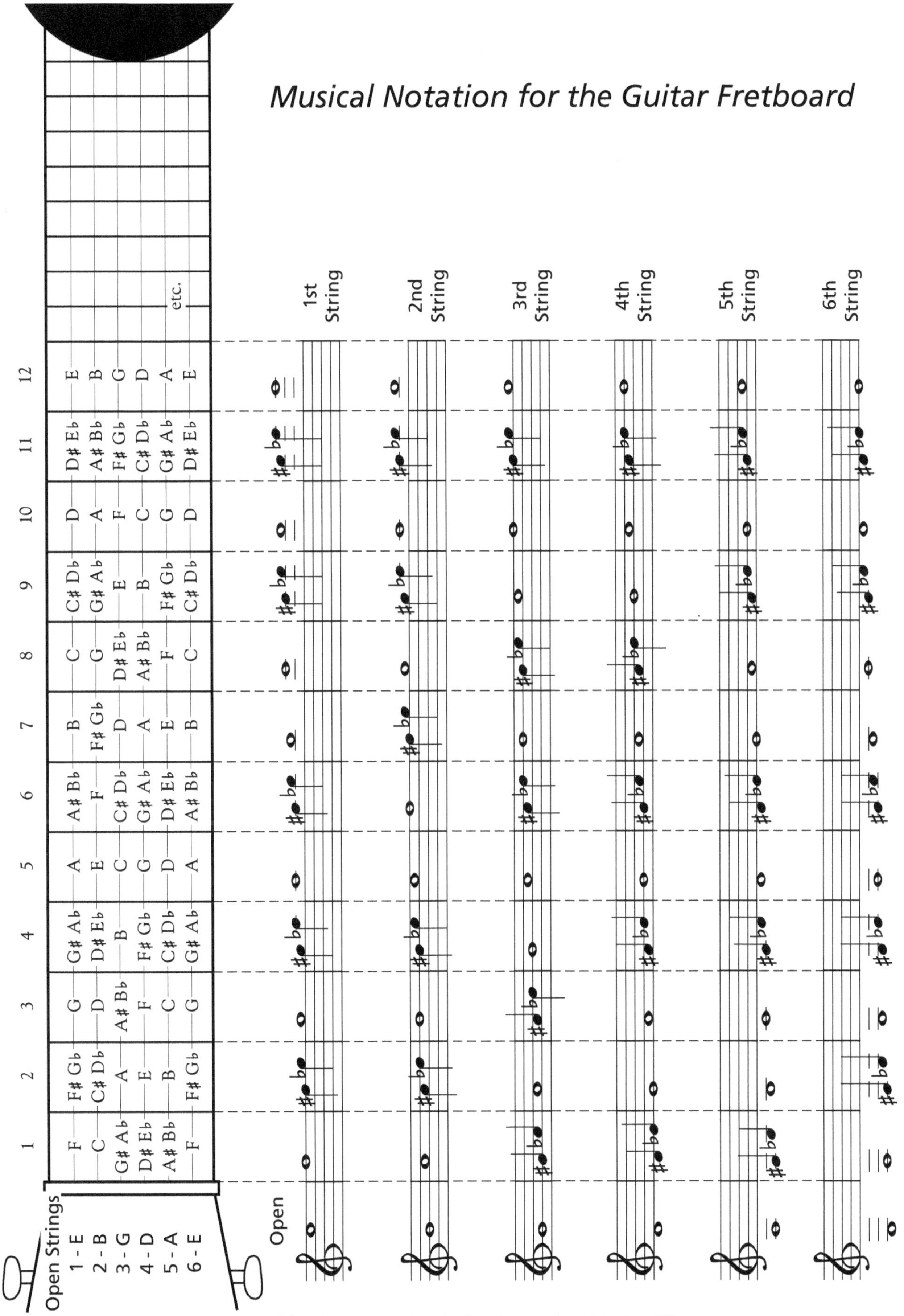

Transposing Chord Progressions

Don L. Davis

Chords are represented by the Key Name and the chord type, e.g. Am = the A minor chord. All chords are designated in this way (seventh, major, minor seventh, etc.), and in the universal key it is shown by a Roman numeral followed by the abbreviation for that chord (e.g., V7 would be a seventh chord based on the fifth tone in the scale). Virtually all musical notation and most musicians use the Roman numeral system (universal key) for writing chord charts and transposing chord progressions.

All of us have run into songs that we liked, but the chord progressions were too hard. To transpose a song from one key to another is an easy and straightforward process.

1. First, *identify the key the song is written in* that you want to change, and *write out its chord progression*:

   Example: F / C7 / F / F / Dm / G7 / C7 / F

2. Now, using the *Table of Keys* scale chart, **write down the scale of the song in its original key** (in this example, the key of **F**) on the **top line** (i.e., "Original Key" line) on your transposing worksheet. Note: For most songs, all you will need is to write down the letters corresponding to the Roman numerals only (called the diatonic scale). For some songs, however, you need to write down all twelve notes (the entire chromatic scale).

3. *Circle all the letters used in the song on the "Original Key" line along with the Roman numerals and other slots directly underneath on the "Universal Key" line.* Don't worry right now about the chord endings, those pesky little suffixes behind the letters (i.e., the "m"s, "major 7"s, "7"s, "9"s, etc.) Just make certain that you *circle all the letters* in the chord progression on both lines!

4. Next, *select the key you will play and sing the song in.* (Get this right; if you get the song too high or low no one can sing it, or if you transpose it to a key you can't play, it's a drag! For this example, let's say you decided to transpose the song from the key of **F** to the key of **C**.)

5. Once you've found the key you want to use, *write down its scale on the "New Key" line*, the bottom line on your transposing sheet. (Again, refer to your *Table of Keys* scale chart.)

6. Now, *circle all the letters on the "New Key" line that match the circles in the original and universal key*. In other words, simply circle all the letters on the bottom row that line up with those on the top two rows. Leave no circle out– **match all the corresponding letters in all three lines**!

7. *Now, rewrite the progression in the new key* by matching the letters in the original progression with their partners in the new key. Match the two, letter for letter, and chord type for chord type. (Now make sure you attach to each letter its chord type suffix, its "m", "7", "maj 7", or whatever. *If you leave these out, the chords won't sound right!*)

   So, here's the transposed progression:
   C / G7 / C / C / Am / D7 / G7 / C

8. You're done. *Enjoy the song in your new key!* Transfer the progression to transparency, create your lead sheet, or whatever! (Be sure to use a capo if necessary for pitch–make it just right, not too high, not too low for you and others to sing!)

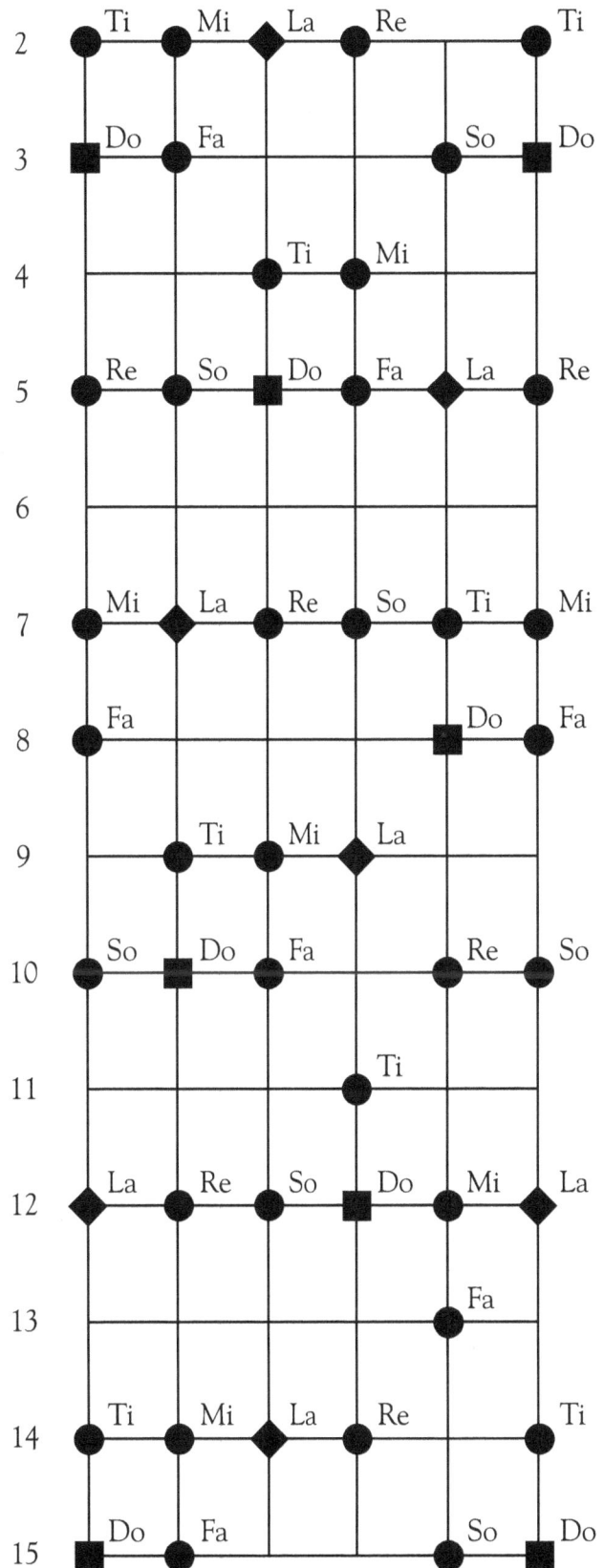

Guitar Accompaniment Guide

**Diatonic Scale
(with corresponding scale degrees)**

Do = 1 (Root/Tonic)

Re = 2

Mi = 3

Fa = 4

So = 5

La = 6 (Minor)

Ti = 7

Do = 8 (Octave)

Rules

1. Practice from ■ to ■ and ◆ to ◆.

2. Practice four frets at a time.

3. Don't fudge on the fingering.

4. Always practice with tempo and beat.

5. "First speed, then accuracy" is WRONG.

6. Eliminate notes for effect.

7. Concentrate on hitting the right note.

8. Listen! Make sure you are going through the scale.

9. Play with music.

Fret					
2	Ti	Mi	La	Re	Ti
3	Do	Fa		So	Do
4			Ti	Mi	
5	Re	So	Do	Fa	La	Re
6					
7	Mi	La	Re	So	Ti	Mi
8	Fa			Do	Fa
9		Ti	Mi	La	
10	So	Do	Fa		Re	So
11				Ti	
12	La	Re	So	Do	Mi	La
13				Fa	
14	Ti	Mi	La	Re	Ti
15	Do	Fa		So	Do

Rhythm Patterns and Riffs:
How to Create and Use Them for Emphasis and Enjoyment
Don L. Davis

Introduction

Welcome to the fascinating world of creating and using rhythm patterns and riffs, some of the most important tools in making your music refreshing and fun!

Riffs are a set pattern of notes that have been placed together for a particular effect. They are usually repeated throughout a song, and often become the means by which you identify a tune. They are useful in composition, adding nuance to your playing, comping (accompanying with a lead play), finding appropriate parts rhythmically for particular voices in a band, and, most importantly, giving your playing and composition your distinctive flavor. Riffs, above all, are fun, and make your playing interesting!

While there are many ways to learn riffs, there are some basic principles which can enable you to become the kind of player that can create, imitate, and sustain patterns of play throughout your music, and provide the kind of interest and relief that is critical in band play.

Baker's Dozen Principles of Riffmaking

1. In order to learn music, concentrate first on mastering rhythms and practicing riffs: to be musical, focus first on rhythmic cool.

The most elemental principles of music in my estimation are beat, pattern, and rhythm. Riffs are essentially patterns playing in a song for effect. They augment and are birthed from rhythmic patterns, so, if you are going to be good at riffing, you must learn to master rhythm. Most of the time young players will ignore the fundamentals of music, to their own detriment. The fundamentals, after all, seem boring to play and practice–they got no punch in 'em! Nothing could be further from the truth. In order to master your instrument, you do not focus on your instrument, but on rhythm and its theory. Once you are comfortable in playing the different rhythms on beat, on time, in tempo, with feeling, then you apply that knowledge to the voice of the instrument which you happen to play. Music, regardless of the style and genre, is a physics kind of thing. No rhythm, no music. No rhythm, no riffs.

2. Above all your getting in musical grasping, concentrate on mastering the downbeat!

The downbeat in my opinion is the critical dimension of rhythm. The great soul singer James Brown talked about the "One," the big accented beat which cycles around in funk and jazz styles. This big, punchy, growling One is the key to most forms of popular music, and can be felt by a listener, though they know nothing of the theory and makeup of musical composition. You feel the downbeat *BEFORE* you know anything about it.

As a player, you must understand that music is a mathematical phenomenon. It demands rules and laws, and functions creatively within tight boundaries. If you understand its dynamics and how they function, you will be able to make wonderful music, beyond what you would have imagined. In order to do this, however, you must become a human metronome; you must master the downbeat and rhythms so well that you do not miss, slip, speed up, slow down, or alter the beat. The beat is inviolate; it must be respected in all playing. Riffs, which seem to be utterly free from all forms of constraint, are actually merely patterns within a rhythmic structure. This sounds like gobbledegook, but it is pretty important. For now, just take my word that you have to master the "One" in order to groove, to give your music structure, and make it enjoyable to the ear.

3. In the music you enjoy, start listening for riffs in the patterns of chords and each instrument and vocal voice.

No matter what the song, every one has a melody, some harmony, tempo, beat, and overall feel. Instruments work together, chording, comping, and accenting one another for effect. When you riff, you focus on contributing with your instrument by concentrating on your voice. You can enhance your ability to play by being a music detective sometimes; concentrate on the voice within a song and see what patterns it is playing. Often, you will get a recurring set of notes, played at a particular time in the song for effect. This is the essence of riffing.

4. Assign your beats to a pattern; connect everything you sing, play, and tap, along with every riff to a particular rhythm pattern or signature.

Riffs demand some kind of rhythmic ticket; in other words, no riff can be played successfully without conforming to a particular pattern set by the tempo and beat of the song. Riffs will often time join in sync with the pattern (for instance, many bass riffs are based on the bass drum of the trap set. The bassist simply plays a lyrical phrase that corresponds to the punch of the bass drum in the trap set.) This is extremely helpful. Voices in song usually correspond to some rhythmic pattern set by the percussion of the band or ensemble. When you think about creating and using riffs, focus first on some rhythmic lick of the drum or percussion you can "sync up" with, and experiment along those lines.

5. Be loopy: learn the "rule of Mr. Eight" and the "power of the One."

As mentioned before, nothing is as critical as learning the power of the one, or the downbeat. Today's popular music is wonderfully predictable, yet possessing a great variety of styles, beats, and genres. Virtually all forms of popular and contemporary music creates phrases and patterns of music and rhythms, and these are repeated every eight beats. This patternizing is now referred to as "looping," and it allows for great innovation in composition and play. Software and music production packages exist which create different samples of music which can be snapped together like Lego toys to create "loops," a musical arrangement of a phrase intended to be repeated every eight beats. This kind of structure is plainly identifiable even to the novice in blues, rock, folk, and country musical styles.

The rule of eight is key for riff making, for it will enable you to "hunker down" on that block of time your riff is created for. Don't get me wrong: riffs can extend from little hiccups for a moment or so, to long solo riffs during solo play. The point is, however, that all riffs evolve, that is, they begin from a deliberate pattern and grow outward.

6. For best results in beat making and keeping, begin with your "mouth" and your "foot."

In learning rhythm (and making progress in the direction of Riffland), one of the greatest tools is your mouth. By making sounds with your mouth, patterns within a rhythmic set, you can create the form of the riff, and later learn its substance. This sounds tough, but it is as easy as humming and tapping your feet.

How many times have you heard a song and followed the melody line with some sound or other that you made with your mouth. You hit the melody line note for note, using your mouth as your "instrument." This is an easy and fun way not only to follow riffs and melodies but also to create them. If you prefer, you can tap out your rhythms with your foot or hand, tapping or drumming out the pattern before you determine what music to use for them.

This simple discipline is key for creating musical riffs. You will typically begin with a pattern, and then you will fill in the stuff and guts of the pattern with sounds and melody and lyrics or whatever. Learn to free yourself up by making your mouth, hands, and feet an integral part of your riff making.

Rhythm Patterns and Riffs, continued

7. Learn from the pros: Start with their stuff, adapt and change it to make it your own.

The pros (those who make their living in music) follow certain patterns that the popular audience pays money to hear. They are able to play well beyond the CDs that we hear, but they will not, because most of the audiences would and could not tolerate listening to their genius unleashed. Rather, then, they play what the popular audiences can enjoy and handle. This is not a patronizing remark. They simply conform to the tastes of the masses, and thus, become the veritable super stars that they are.

Nothing succeeds like success, and so you can detect riffs in popular music, and learn to imitate and expand your musical knowledge through them. You need not woodenly follow them, or lament that you cannot play the solo they can. The point here is to learn the art of comping (riffing) in order to create and use your own.

Modern music provides a near-endless supply of learning how accomplished musicians learn to play riffs to enhance the effect of their sound. Spend not a little time listening to the pros, and borrow from them much! There is much to learn from them.

8. "Taking it slow is the way to go!": Slow patterns down to learn them well.

Riffs, especially difficult ones which extend beyond two measures to eight, twelve, or more, can only be learned slowly. When learning a riff, play it slowly. Look at what the riff demands of you physically, what notes you'll have to hit, the dynamics of the music to be played, and how you want to nuance it. In order to *PLAY* something freely, with speed and excellence, it must be *LEARNED* slowly, dully, in a plodding way until it is mastered. While that may be a tad bit over spoken, it is largely true.

9. Do it again and again, only differently: Learn the turnaround rules of modern music.

When you find a riff you like, you are in the house (that is, you are in a great situation!) Typically, riffs are repeated at various positions for effect (this is especially true for rhythm instruments, the "pocket" keepers–piano, bass, drums, and percussion). Once you have a pattern of notes you believe are melodically strong, in key, and can be rhythmically done for effect in a song, then try playing the same riff in the fourth and fifth positions, or its relative minor key, in the second and third positions. You usually have to augment a riff for time's sake, and so some variation must be made to make the turnaround in time for the root tone. Still, this is a good practice. Learn to play your riffs in different positions and at different times. The overall nuance of the song can be greatly affected by this.

10. Create interest by playing patterns up and down the scale.

This is related to the last point, and simply re-inforces it. Sometimes you can riff in step intervals down or up, or half intervals down or up for effect at certain moments of the song. Experimentation is the key. The rule of thumb of music is this: If you don't like it, don't play it. You're under no obligation to play stuff you don't like or find interesting. But don't be a fuddy-duddy. Experiment first.

11. Variety is the spice of life: Vary effects by altering tempo, beat, intensity, and sustain.

Just a little variation in your riff at certain times and in certain ways can greatly enhance your song's overall impact. By altering the dynamics of your riff (e.g., slowing it down or speeding it up, sustaining notes or altering the pattern slightly) you will create an entirely new feel, which is critical for your playing enjoyment.

Rhythm Patterns and Riffs, *continued*

Am I emphasizing enjoyment too much? Naw! Musical delight is a big part of musicianship, and keeping your music and play interesting and enjoyable is critical to keeping your music excellent and superior. It is amazing how simple changes in minor things can so dramatically impact what you learn and how you continue to play. So, vary your riff sometime and see if that helps you with new ideas and ways to enhance your play.

12. Create your own library of sound: write down and/or record your riffs for reference.

"The dullest pencil is sharper than the most brilliant mind." That might be a little overstated, but the point is made. Once you create a riff you like, pop in a cassette and record it, or write it out in tablature or score. If you can't play it yet, hum it into the cassette. One way or another, you ought to find a way to record your riffs for future reference.

13. Finally, have fun and experiment by employing your riff patterns in songs.

This is the most creative part. You ought to use your riffs in your songs, play, composition, and practice. This is the only way to make the riff your own, and cement it into your mind and soul. Repeated practice of the riff will make the playing of it involuntary, and you'll be able to pull it out whenever you as a player believe it is important. Remember, riffs are simply patterns or phrases of music in rhythm designed to enhance the overall effect of a song. That is fancy talk to say that once you learn a ton of riffs, you can throw them in (let me change that metaphor) you can tastefully include them into the musical stew you're brewing up at that time. And won't it be tasty to the other members of the band, and the people who are enjoying the sounds of the music you're dishing up.

Remember the power of the "One!"

And the Beat Goes On
Strumming: Making Your Guitar a Rhythm Machine
Don L. Davis

Strumming:
Getting a Feel for a Steady Pulse

Of all instruments around, the guitar is one of the premiere rhythm machines. When played with sensitivity and passion, you can get every possible kind of emotion from a guitar. A good rhythm guitar is essential for worship and praise music (at least according to my mind!), and learning a few rules will make this not only possible but enjoyable, too.

Strumming is primarily about the sound you want, the flavor the song requires, and your ability to be regular. By varying different elements of a strum, you create a rhythm feel, a kind of overall sense of the song (passionate, laid back, basic, complex, etc.). The definition of a strum is a chord played at a particular speed with a given number of strums associated with that chord. Strumming is related to time in music, and strumming patterns emphasize this relationship.

A strum can be compared to a clock ticking off seconds. The space between each 'tick' of a clock is equal to every other space between 'ticks.' The space between each strum has also been equal. This is what they have in common. The second on a clock is a measurement of time passing, and so far, we can create strums that emphasize this unit of time. Whether you play a progression fast or slow, you must measure the time each chord is to be played by how many strums you give it. A strum consists of a set number of strums of a chord at a particular speed.

We vary strums by varying the speed in which they are played, the patterns we use when we play the chords, and the length of time we give to each strum in the pattern. The easiest way to understand strumming is the creation of a pattern according to time, with certain chords and certain hand move-ments with each chord. Strumming is like

percussion; if you can keep time with a stick, you can probably learn to strum. The more advanced your rhythm abilities, the more variation you can give to your strumming.

The goal in strumming is keeping time with your instrument. In strumming we have to learn how to measure time in music so we can know when to change chords and when we want to vary the patterns to play different strums.

Beat, Pulse, Tempo:
The Get-Down Mechanics of Music

In order to strum well, you simply must strive to master the elements associated with keeping time in music. Below are the biggies to understand.

BEAT: A single throb in music. The downbeat is the bread-and-butter of any song, and mastering the beat is essential to keeping time, playing with others, and making music. You can keep the beat by strumming, tapping your foot, or making sounds with your mouth.

PULSE: This is a steady repeated beat. When you get a beat and repeat it with regularity and intensity you create the pulse. This may be subdued (as in a classical piece) or driving, (as in a rousing rock-and-roll ballad). An example of a pulse is the tick-tock regularity of an old non-digital clock. The seconds on a clock repeat in this way. Your heart performs its job this way (the doctor takes your pulse by counting the number of beats in a certain amount of time.)

What's wonderful about music is that once you get the pulse, you can allow silence to work its way into music. When the beat is clear and you know it, you can allow no sound to play from your instrument, but you have not lost the beat or pulse. The overall pulse is there, whether you are playing your instrument or not. Great variation and fun can be had when you learn the importance of counting and staying with the pulse in your playing.

TEMPO: A tempo represents the particular speed of the pulse or beat. Tempo measures how fast or slow the beat is, or technically, precisely how many beats per minute the song requires. There are a lot of fancy sounding Italian names associated with various tempos, which are not critical to know. What is important is the ability to master the instrument well enough that you can play comfortably at the tempo demanded by the song. You should not be surprised that when you first learn chord changes that you will not be able to make them cleanly when you first begin to play. After you become more comfortable with the guitar, you will see that you will get better at making the chord changes, and as a result, your strumming will become more on beat. You will be able to strum faster, with greater variation, and with effortless mastery, using silence and variation to create a pleasant overall sound in your playing. Take heart, it's coming!

MEASURE: A collection of beats according to a definite pattern. What is wonderful about a strum is that you can program a strum according to a particular beat, or combine two measures and create a unique strum. The strum does not have to be on each beat, and you can have any number of beats per measure. As with the strum, repeating the same number of beats per measure creates a unique pattern.

BAR LINE: This is a vertical line on scoring sheets used to divide the music into equal repeating groups of beats. They are usually divided into groups of two, three, four, six, or eight.

TIME SIGNATURE: Two numbers stacked on top of each other. This is noted at a song's beginning to tell how many beats each measure will receive during the song. The bottom number indicates the amount of time that each beat in the measure represents, and the top number represents the number of beats per measure, that is, how many beats have been grouped into each measure. Inches are placed into larger groups called "feet"; as inches are to feet, so beats are grouped into measures. 4/4 says, then, that there will be four beats in a measure.

Let's wrap this up. A beat is a single throb or sound, and if it is repeated in a regular, steady, ongoing pattern it is called a pulse. The pulse can move at a fast, medium, or slow pace or speed which is called the tempo, which is counted in a group of beats called a measure which has a bar line which shows the measure and its beats in a score, on paper. The time signature informs us just how many beats per measure the song is written in.

This talk about time is the key to strumming, and the key to music itself. If you want to be good at your instrument, at worship leading, and at music itself, determine to become a master at the art of the beat and the pulse. "And the beat goes on!"

Tasty Rhythm Practice: Two Stacks of Pies

One of the easiest ways to master rhythm is to divide its beats up into various segments using the names of pies. Sounding out the names represents the division of the beats. Below are two columns of measures with beats contained within them. Play, sound, or tap these beats out, column by column, paying attention to the divisions (the pie soundings)

as you go. For instance, for the "Apple" measure you would sound, "Pie - apple - pie - pie" by either counting, tapping, or singing as you play. Once you master the division, you may substitute all beats in the measure for that pie (e.g., instead of "Pie - apple - pie - pie" you would say "Apple - apple - apple - apple," maintaining the right tempo).

Pie

Chocolate

Apple

Gooseberry

Jerky

Butterscotch

Orange

Banana

Huckleberry

Peppermint

Learning to Apply the "Pies" to the Strum Process
Don L. Davis

What is critical in learning to strum efficiently is learning to play chords strongly, on time, according to a particular predetermined pattern. This definition is what strumming is. When done well, your strum is on beat, on pulse, at the right tempo, playing the chords cleanly and strongly, following a particular pattern that is in sync with the time signature of the song, and the flavor of the melody.

Sound like a lot to know? It's not at all! As a matter of fact, if you are able to play the chords well, stay on beat, and keep the pattern going, you will become a champion strummer!

The rules of thumb are clear for great strumming. Let me repeat them.

PLAYING CHORDS CLEANLY AND STRONGLY
You finger the chords correctly, and when you strum, it sounds full and clear.

PLAYING THE CHORDS ON TIME (PULSE)
You play the chords correctly but within the time frame of the measure and at the speed of the tempo being played.

PLAYING THE CHORDS IN A RECURRING PATTERN
Strumming is nothing but loops applied to the guitar. All good strums are essentially no more than a certain rhythmic pattern set down and repeated over and over. By definition, if you do not have a recurring pattern that repeats, you do not have a strum. When you strum, you are following a pattern of up/down strokes which repeat every number of beats.

When learning to strum, one of the most helpful ways is to use the "pies" of rhythm to experiment with different strum patterns for your playing. In other words, each "beat" can be subdivided into various sections (the most common being either two, three, or four sections) and strums associated with each of these pie divisions. For instance, Strum #1 involves strumming one strum per beat, while Strum #2 involves strumming twice for each beat. As you become proficient at keeping time on tempo, playing chords correctly, and following patterns faithfully, you can try more and more different kinds of "pies" to create more and more unique rhythms. Be careful, though! What you are looking for are clean, crisp, and correct strums at the lower speeds, easier chording, and basic patterns. Once you master the easier strums, you'll be ready to graduate to more difficult materials, chord voicings, livelier tempos, and more complex patterns.

Hold on–there'll be plenty of time for growth. Master the easier strums first!

In the next few pages you will learn some very basic strums. Pay careful attention how these strums follow the rules of thumb above.

Strums

Strum #1. This is the most basic strum. It involves strumming once at the beginning of each beat.

Strum #2. This pattern involves both down and *up* strums. Go slowly here. In strum #2 you will play *two strums per beat*, the first strum down and the second strum up. When do you play these strums? How do they relate to our "beats"?

To learn how to play more than one strum in each beat, and still play at a regular, even tempo (and with the right number of beats), we need to know a bit more about time measurement, *on paper*.

Let's look at a swinging pendulum. . . . The pendulum swings back and forth at whatever speed we set it. It can go fast or slow. A beat is one complete swing from point A to point B and back to A again.

Now let's turn that pendulum sideways. (Ignore the fact that gravity would not allow this to take place.)

Now we're going to spread out the swing of our pendulum, so we can see it more easily on paper.

Let's compare the motion of our pendulum to the beats . . .

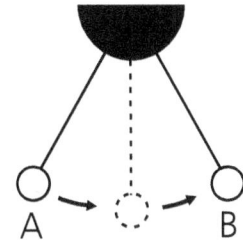

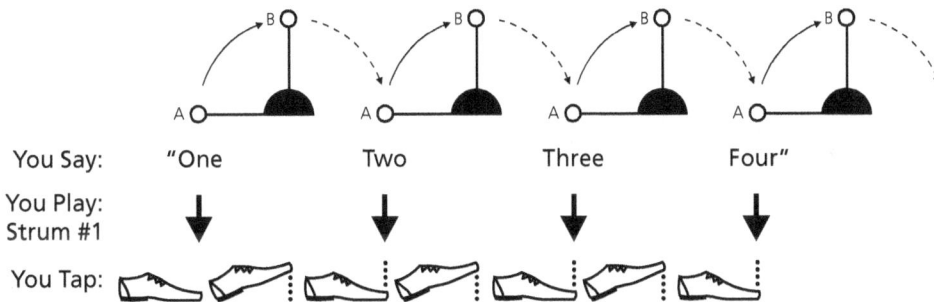

You Say:	"One	Two	Three	Four"
You Play: Strum #1				

In Strum #1 you strummed down once at the *beginning* of each beat.

You know that between every DOWN strum you make, you have to bring your hand *up* again to get ready for the next DOWN strum. The same holds true for your foot tapping. Every time you tap, you have to raise your foot *up* to tap again. Let's look at Strum #1 again with the pendulum, and all of these extra up motions.

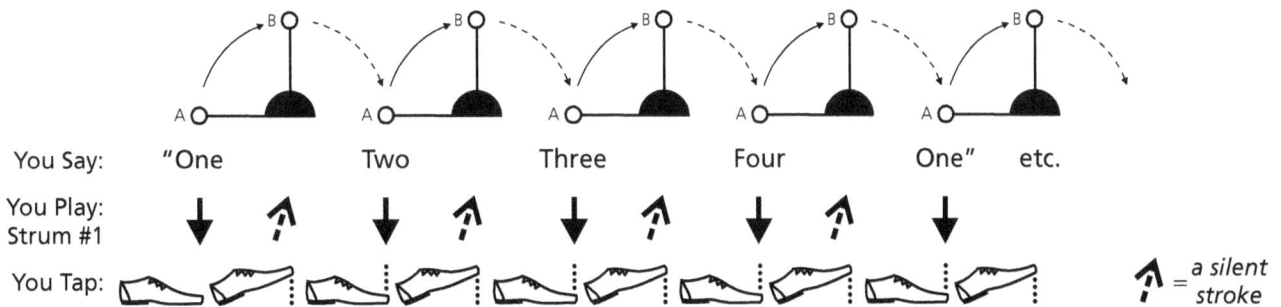

You Say:	"One	Two	Three	Four	One" etc.
You Play: Strum #1					

↗ = a silent stroke

Strums, continued

Somewhere in the middle of each beat you are bringing your hand and foot back up again to get ready to strum down. Our pendulum shows exactly where the *halfway point* is on each beat. This is important if you're going to play a repeating pattern in which you bring your hand *up* at the same place each time. (Knowing the halfway point helps you keep track of *when* to bring your hand up . . .) Try the pattern shown above but with a new "wrinkle." Strum on the down *and up* motions. You could count it like this:

| You Say: | "One | and | Two | and | Three | and | Four | and | One | and" | etc. |
| You Play: Strum #2 | Down ↓ | Up ↑ | Down ↓ | Up ↑ | Down ↓ | Up ↑ | Down ↓ | Up ↑ | Down ↓ | Up ↑ | etc. |

The new notation for this strumming will be ⎏. It means two strums per *beat*, one at the beginning and one at the *halfway point*.

Strum Two

| You Say: | "One | and | Two | and | Three | and | Four | and | One | and" | etc. |

4 beats per measure -
(strumming 8 times)
(strum down, then up)

3 beats per measure -
(strumming 6 times)

2 beats per measure -
(strumming 4 times)

Strums, continued

We don't have to strum on every beat and every halfway point. Let's try some new strums, using our new notation. (Remember your hand will go up and down here *whether* or *not* you hit the string.)

Strum Three. Repeat this pattern using your A chord.

4 beats per measure -

1   2   3   4   1   2   3   4

3 beats per measure -

1   2 and 3   1   2 and 3   1   2 and 3

2 beats per measure -

1   2 and   1   2 and   1   2 and

Notice that in a four beat measure you hit the strings in a pattern - down, down up, down, down up. In a three beat pattern, it goes down, down up, down. For a two beat pattern, it also alternated down, down up.

Strum Four. This is a four and three beat pattern only. A two beat pattern is the same as Strum 3.

4 beats per measure -

1   2   3   4   1   2   3   4

3 beats per measure -

1   2   3   1   2   3

Strum Five. This is a four and three beat pattern. A two beat pattern would be the same as Strum 1.

4 beats per measure -

1   2   3   4   1   2   3   4

3 beats per measure -

1   2   3   1   2   3

Learn each of these patterns. Try them with the progressions below. Beware–do not rush–try to keep your eye on the page.

1.   E/A/E

2.   D/D7/G/A/A7/D

3.   D/E7/A/D

4.   A/D/A/E7/A

5.   G/Am7/D7/G

6.   Em/Am7/Em

Varying Your Strum to Enhance Your Playing

Varying your strum pattern will enhance your guitar chord playing tremendously. Beginning guitarists all seem to "lock in" to a single pattern and tempo, playing every song in the same way. This makes their playing predictable and monotonous. In order to give variety to your playing, practice your strumming work by changing the *number* and *division* of your strums per chord or beat.

The "pie" system of rhythm is very helpful in learning new strum patterns. Instead of giving each chord or beat a single strum (e.g., "pie"), why not try two strums per beat ("apple") or even three strums ("chocolate") per chord or beat. Or you might vary the beat by interchanging the beat patterns together (pie - apple - apple - chocolate). However you change the patterns of strumming your guitar, always make certain that you 1) play your strums evenly, 2) keep your strumming on time and in tempo, and 3) play the chords correctly, sounding them out loudly and clearly.

Now play three strums per chord.

1. E | A | E ‖
    /// | /// | ///

2. D | D7 | G | A | A7 | D ‖
    /// | /// | /// | /// | /// | ///

3. D | E7 | A | D ‖
    /// | /// | /// | ///

4. A | D | A | E7 | A ‖
    /// | /// | /// | /// | ///

5. G | Am7 | D7 | G ‖
    /// | /// | /// | ///

6. Em | Am7 | Em ‖
    /// | /// | ///

1. E | A | E ‖
    // | // | //

2. E | D7 | G | A | A7 | D ‖
    // | // | // | // | // | //

3. D | E7 | A | D ‖
    // | // | // | //

4. A | D | A | E7 | A ‖
    // | // | // | // | //

5. Em | Am7 | Em ‖
    // | // | //

How to Use Rhythm Practice Charts

Practicing your rhythms is the surest and easiest way to learn how to make keeping the beats natural and satisfying. The following charts were designed to help you learn how to master the fundamentals of rhythm in an interesting but challenging way. The numbers running down the left side of the chart are exercise numbers, and the "dots" represent the hits or taps you will make as you count your way across (numbers 1-8 at the top of the chart). Choose a tempo for your practice session (slow, medium, or fast paced beat). While tapping out or sounding out the grayed-in numbers (1, 3, 5, 7) with your foot, hit or tap with your hand the "dots" at the time indicated in the chart. The key is tapping the dots at the right time while you maintain a steady beat in the grayed-in portion.

This is a challenge–in other words, as the exercises progress, it ain't easy! Always seek to master a rhythm at a slower pace, and increase the difficulty of your playing by picking up the pace of the tempo. Concentrate on playing well, not playing fast. Fast will come if good comes along with him!

The blank charts are included so you can create your own exercises to play with or share with others.

Rhythm Practice Chart #1

	1	+	2	+	3	+	4	+	5	+	6	+	7	+	8	+
1			●		●		●						●		●	
2	●			●	●		●		●		●					
3	●			●	●						●		●			
4		●			●				●					●	●	●
5			●		●						●		●			
6	●	●	●				●		●	●	●				●	
7	●		●		●		●		●		●		●		●	
8			●				●				●				●	
9	●	●	●	●			●		●		●	●			●	
10	●				●	●	●	●	●					●	●	●
11		●	●	●			●	●			●	●			●	●
12	●			●	●						●		●			
13		●			●				●	●	●	●				
14	●	●			●	●			●	●	●	●				
15			●			●	●	●	●				●			
16			●		●				●		●			●		
17	●		●	●	●				●		●	●	●			
18	●		●		●		●	●			●			●	●	
19			●				●				●				●	
20	●	●		●	●		●		●	●	●	●			●	
21		●			●	●				●				●	●	
22	●			●	●						●		●			
23	●		●		●		●		●		●		●		●	

Tempo: _____

Rhythm Practice Chart #2

	1	+	2	+	3	+	4	+	5	+	6	+	7	+	8	+
1	●	●	●			●		●		●			●		●	
2		●	●			●		●	●	●				●		●
3	●								●		●	●			●	●
4	●			●	●			●	●		●	●				●
5	●						●		●		●	●				●
6			●	●			●	●			●	●			●	●
7	●			●		●					●		●			●
8	●	●			●				●	●			●	●		
9						●	●			●	●			●	●	
10	●		●	●	●		●	●	●		●	●	●		●	●
11		●	●	●		●	●	●		●	●	●		●	●	●
12	●	●			●	●	●	●	●	●		●	●	●		●
13	●		●			●			●		●	●		●	●	
14		●			●		●	●			●	●		●	●	
15		●				●			●			●		●		●
16		●			●	●			●	●	●		●		●	
17	●	●	●			●	●			●			●		●	●
18			●				●		●	●		●	●		●	●
19	●	●	●	●		●	●		●	●		●	●	●		●
20		●		●		●				●		●		●		
21	●		●	●			●	●			●	●			●	
22	●		●			●	●		●		●		●		●	
23		●			●		●		●		●	●	●	●		●

Tempo: _____

Rhythm Practice Chart #3

	1	+	2	+	3	+	4	+	5	+	6	+	7	+	8	+
1	●			●			●			●			●	●	●	
2	●			●		●	●	●		●			●		●	
3	●			●		●		●		●	●	●			●	●
4	●	●				●	●			●	●	●				●
5	●				●	●				●	●				●	
6		●			●			●			●			●	●	
7		●	●			●	●	●		●	●			●	●	●
8	●	●		●			●			●	●		●		●	
9		●	●	●		●	●			●	●		●	●	●	
10	●			●			●		●			●			●	
11		●	●			●		●		●	●			●		●
12	●				●		●				●			●	●	
13		●				●	●			●				●	●	
14	●	●		●	●			●		●		●	●			
15			●		●	●			●		●			●	●	●
16				●			●					●			●	
17	●	●			●	●			●	●			●	●		
18		●	●			●	●		●			●		●	●	
19		●		●			●	●		●				●	●	
20		●	●	●		●	●	●		●	●	●			●	
21	●				●				●	●	●		●	●		●
22		●		●	●	●		●		●		●	●		●	
23		●			●		●		●		●	●				

Tempo: _____

Rhythm Practice Chart

	1	✛	2	✛	3	✛	4	✛	5	✛	6	✛	7	✛	8	✛
1																
2																
3																
4																
5																
6																
7																
8																
9																
10																
11																
12																
13																
14																
15																
16																
17																
18																
19																
20																
21																
22																
23																

Tempo: _____

Rhythm Practice Chart

	1	+	2	+	3	+	4	+	1	+	2	+	3	+	4	+
1																
2																
3																
4																
5																
6																
7																
8																
9																
10																
11																
12																
13																
14																
15																
16																
17																
18																
19																
20																
21																
22																
23																

Tempo: _____

Rhythm Practice Chart

	1	✛	2	✛	3	✛	4	✛	5	✛	6	✛
1												
2												
3												
4												
5												
6												
7												
8												
9												
10												
11												
12												
13												
14												
15												
16												
17												
18												
19												
20												
21												
22												
23												

Tempo: _____

Rhythm Practice Chart

	1	✛	2	✛	3	✛	1	✛	2	✛	3	✛
1												
2												
3												
4												
5												
6												
7												
8												
9												
10												
11												
12												
13												
14												
15												
16												
17												
18												
19												
20												
21												
22												
23												

Tempo: _____

www.ingramcontent.com/pod-product-compliance
Lightning Source LLC
Chambersburg PA
CBHW081539040426

42447CB00014B/3438